I Have Secrets

Adrienne Cosgrave

I Have Secrets

To my beloved
Rick
(1963–2010)
and to my sisters,
my brothers
and my parents,
whose love and support
has always been unconditional

I Have Secrets
ISBN 978 1 76041 925 7
Copyright © Adrienne Cosgrave 2020

First published 2020 by
Ginninderra Press
PO Box 3461 Port Adelaide 5015
www.ginninderrapress.com.au

Contents

Trust	7
Grief	8
Bliss	9
New	10
Island	11
Bereft	12
Valentine	13
Tiff	14
Theft	15
Teen	16
Phoenix	17
Over	18
Idol	19
Complicated	20
Breathe	21
2019	22
Blue	24
Breakdown	25
Drunk	26
Faith	27
Fleeting	28
Fox	29
Melodrama	30
Pattern	31
Wed	32
Bubba	33
Widow	34

Trust

I have secrets.

Words unspoken,
idle fancies,
distant voices and hidden selves.

Spiders scuttling through sliding doors,
bloodied notions
and petal-pink dreams.

Were they to fall,
ivory pearls,
into your hands,
could you maintain their lustre?

Or would you scatter, strew and expose
to be stomped
under strange boots?

Perhaps you might string them together
and hold them close;
a mystery to consider,
a rosary to believe.

We all have secrets.
It's really a matter of trust.

Grief

I am adrift without you.

My thoughts meander
through the waft and curl
of cigarette smoke,
slipping in and out of shadows,
crouching in a cobwebbed corner
and sifting through the piles of memories
we can no longer share.

I am out of circulation
and down for the count.

Forget Jack.

I am my own broken
       lonely
       heart
and miss is far too small a word.

You died.
I cried.

I'm crying still.

Bliss

Tonight
I shake the ghosts
from my shoulders,
where they hang
whispering deadly blessings
in my ear.

Beneath your hands,
their grey transparency
flakes away
and falls,
dry and dusty,
at your feet.

I want only
to wrap my name
around your wrist
so I can move with your pulse.
I want to unravel,
until we're speaking in tongues,
spirits aflame,
a fusion of bliss.

Tonight
I shed my skin,
surrendering all my secrets
to your silent touch.

New

It's so easy to wake
with your smile on my face
and your sighs on my tongue

and I'm back, running with laughter
and watching the beach run;
a child's hope in my hand
and your heart in my pocket.

I live in the wake of your fingertips
and we shine –
resolute –
against this sometime dark ceiling
without a star.

Island

Remember when we were young
and beautiful
and ruled the world?

We spent days basking in the glow
of our concentrated heat.

Nothing could touch us.
We shared stories and songs.
We were indulgent
        hedonistic
          complete.

And love was our island.

Bereft

More than 3,000 days

and with no witness,
I am master of my own isolation.

I am shrinking;
folding in on myself
like a paper puzzle.

I have history and memory enough
to go through the motions;
distractions to pass the time.

Everyone thinks I'm real.

My life is a mirage
and I am a ghost passing through it;
sensed, but untouched.

I am a body
dumped in the river,
all those mixed blessings
weighing me down,
my arm outstretched
and moving gently with the current,

waving,
ever so slightly,
in the hope
that I might be found.

Valentine

I dream of you often.
We meet by chance.
You are sometimes elusive,
but never dismissive
and always kind.

And I wake, snug and wistful in my morning cocoon
wondering…

If we were to pass in the street,
would you notice?
Would you call?
Would you dream of me too?

Tiff

Some days I'd like to blow your head off
with one single scream
and send all our yesterdays
out the back door
in a mad telephone rush.

I can hear your skeletons rattling
over the line
and I'm left hanging,
29 pieces of silver strewn at my feet,
still wondering what the fuck it is
I'm supposed to have done.

Seems like it's all or nothing with us.

They say it's no fun
living on in-betweens
and anyway, we're on extremes;

so beware the little creatures inside your head

and stay close tonight.

Theft

Death stole you.

A strawberry thief.
So quick,
so sly,
so precise.

The perfect crime.
And right before my eyes.

Death stole you
like the ocean steals the shore,
drawing you in,
pulling you under.

And our boys,
just babies really,
waking to find you gone
forever.

No returns.
No refunds.
No recourse.
No redemption.

Death stole you
like a carnival conman
and hung us out to dry.

Game over.

What a gyp.

Teen

I've been soaking myself
in a voice
I don't belong to;

spinning by the skin of my teeth
like some skeleton-tipped
strung-out yo-yo.

Please keep me in mind
with your methods of dance and drink.

I want you
to wipe the sadness from my skin.

And you know you kill me
with that sometimenotnownotever smile,

but I need to cling to something.

Phoenix

My reflection
sparkles
in the very centre of your eyes.

Time away from time
and only we exist.

Merging skin
with fragments of breath,
running in tandem
along sweet musk sheets.

I have caught the laughter
in the corners of your smile
that makes this half-body whole;
my senses rippling
to waves of light,

spinning
all to one whiteness,

as we rise,
clear as gods,
above the ashes.

Over

Your discontent
is stifling;

a blistering heat
bouncing off summer concrete.

My throat rasps
under its judgement.

My smile falters.

I have not the will any more.

You – scratching away at dead skin;

and me – a handful of stray prayers
strung around my neck.

We are an arid northerly
blown straight from the desert;
parched and drought-stricken.

Our hope is dust.

Idol

I carry you with me,
under my skin,
in the back of my mind;
my zodiac matchmake,
photos and relics.

Turning over the words
they said you said you said
      nothing to me,

but I could feel and touch your breath
all the same.

Is this some kind of love?

Complicated

A life created
        celebrated
insulated
        propagated
accommodated
        assimilated
inundated
        adulterated
agitated
        isolated
medicated
        brecciated
fabricated
        illuminated
contemplated
        evaluated
authenticated
        appreciated
vindicated
        venerated.

Breathe

Now dying slowly,
slowly,

something unholy
breathes in shadowed silence;
ever present, but not quite real.

Origami butterfly.

Papier mâché love balloon,
too heavy to rise
above its wants.

And I want Forever
to place me in your hands.

I want you
to be my first and last breath,
that I might breathe eternally
in your pictures of living.

2019

The city makes me jumpy.
It holds an unsettling edge.

And I'm caught in the crawl and sprawl,
the surge and splurge.
Trapped heat,
sharp angles,
cold corners.

My nerves are tangled,
my senses skewed.

Hemmed in by grinding gears
and random roadkill,
rush and grab traffic,
the churn and burn of media.

Wedged tight between
jaded teens
and trending professionals.

Me-time mums
with organic kids
and facebook families;
conversation reduced to a series
of words without vowels
and an endless stream
of scripted realities
and PC distortion.

Dogs yapping.
Phones ringing.
Doors slamming.
Too big.
Too loud.
Too fast.

If I step outside, I know what I'll see.
One more stranger seeking celebrity
and another fat arse in lycra.

Blue

I am no one from nowhere
A sigh on the wind
A whisper in the dark
A raindrop caught in the curl of a leaf
A voice out of the blue
My words written in water

Perhaps I am everyone

Breakdown

I awoke to a voice
at the core of my self;
I peeled away layers,
became someone else
and I followed a whisper away from you.

I felt insubstantial,
with you looming large;
barely a glimmer
by your rising star,
so I followed a whisper away from you.

I ran into shadows
and toyed with the night;
I tossed out my prayers
and squeezed my eyes tight.

I sought solace in strangers,
found lips that weren't yours;
I broke my mind
to settle a score;
when a whisper led me away from you.

With a fierce manic power
guiding my hand,
I fell in with forces
I couldn't withstand.

And a thick, spongy sadness
took root in my bones,
I gathered my sorries
and made my way home.
To you.

Drunk

Being with you
is like murder in the dark,
lining up for detention,
walking on eggshells,
a mozzie bite itch
that runs under your skin.

You make everything loud.

You play the diehard,
the blowhard,
the victim,
the thief.

And I curl into myself,
small and quiet,
holding my breath
until you pass out.

Faith

This once
I truly tampered with your ego.

You've bruised mine often
in small, careless ways.

We are each of us flawed,
sticky with insecurities
and promises mislaid.

We could burn it all now
but for one simple truth.

Fleeting

Your voice
is the one perfect
and clear thing.

I'd like to wrap it around
my lonesome body;
Easter sunshine to warm my bones.

Capture it in a jar
to relieve sad silences;

or wear it as a charm
to dispel the rogue doubts
that mill about my feet
like cats waiting to be fed.

If you would only say my name,
walk me home through the mean streets
and cherish an uncertain smile.
We could share our secrets
and know each other every inch;
be triumphant into old age.

I'm looking at you
and I'm looking for love,
but you're looking past me
to somebody else.

Fox

for my mother

There are small treasures
within the gridwork of suburbia.

The whoosh of bats across a darkening sky.
The neighbour's cat,
sleek and silent,
stalking like a professional.

The twist of gold in an autumn leaf
and the weight of raindrops
on a petal.

Or a stately red fox,
burnished in the sunlight,
pausing for a moment,
before disappearing over the fence
into the yard next door.

Melodrama

The lack of you leaves me
pining and restless.

How slowly the night moves,
dragging my heart
along its rough and gravelly
tick-tock road.

I left my soul behind
at our last meeting.
It was lying in the palm of your hand.
You tossed it aside – indifferent.
You let me go – easy peasy.

I hope you know big man
that you broke a girl.

Now I wait by the phone,
pasting together the scraps
of warmth we shared.

Nothing comes from something
and some things never change.

You won't call.
I don't exist
and you're just a shadow.
I'm in love with love.

Pattern

Today
I am inadequate;
a miscarriage in your head.

You hide your love
and bare your scars.

Your perception is my reality.

So I retreat
into the silence of our maze,
wandering,
wondering,
fearing the worst,
knowing the best,
while you play sad and lonely
break-up songs
to manipulate our future.

There is a pattern to us.
Exaltation.
Decimation.

Tomorrow I will be queen.

I guess that's just how we roll.

Wed

dressed for success
in our wedding best
our happiness true
our home is blessed
you love with a love
that outshines the rest
and when you asked me
yes
        I said
yes
        always
yes

Bubba

A remarkable thing.
A miracle thing.
From the kick inside
to the punch of reality;
the first rush of air
to the twitch and pout of your sleep.

I want to throw a witchy white light
to protect you always.

Still,
there are days I could buckle
under your feather weight.

How can one so tiny wield such clout?

Like some half-starved alley cat
spoiling for a fight,
your cries pierce my dreams.
You mark your territory
and stake your claim.

I am slave to the jolt of instinct.
For better and worse,
you own my soul.

Widow

I was different once,
before you left;
there was a whole to me.

Not that anyone can tell;
I am Dorian on the outside.

Still and silent,
while the lives of others
roll around me;
        unabated
                unabridged
                        unaware.

Time means nothing.

I watch it slide by;
raindrops on a windscreen
        beading
                swelling
                        pooling
                              gone.

I only know it exists
because our boys grow;
taller, deeper;
nursing their loss as a shield against incomers.

And I spread alone
Into middle age;
harbouring dreams of impossible love

and tiptoe on the rim
of a hollow
so hollow
I could drop right in and never be found.

www.ingramcontent.com/pod-product-compliance
Lightning Source LLC
Chambersburg PA
CBHW062207100526
44589CB00014B/1999